VICTORIAN GOODS AND MERCHANDISE

2,300 ILLUSTRATIONS

Selected and Arranged by

CAROL BELANGER GRAFTON

DOVER PUBLICATIONS, INC.

Mineola, New York

Copyright

Copyright © 1997 by Dover Publications, Inc.
All rights reserved under Pan American and International Copyright Conventions.

Published in Canada by General Publishing Company, Ltd., 30 Lesmill Road, Don Mills, Toronto, Ontario.
Published in the United Kingdom by Constable and Company, Ltd., 3 The Lanchesters, 162–164 Fulham Palace Road, London W6 9ER.

Bibliographical Note

Victorian Goods and Merchandise: 2,300 Illustrations is a new work, first published by Dover Publications, Inc., in 1997. The selection and arrangement of the illustrations are by Carol Belanger Grafton.

DOVER *Pictorial Archive* SERIES

Library of Congress Cataloging-in-Publication Data

Victorian goods and merchandise : 2,300 illustrations / selected and arranged by Carol Belanger Grafton.
    p.   cm. — (Dover pictorial archive series)
  ISBN 0-486-29698-9 (pbk.)
    1. Decoration and ornament, Victorian. 2. Consumer goods—Miscellanea. 3. Clip art. I. Grafton, Carol Belanger.
II. Series
NK1378.V5 1997
745.2–dc21   97–15501
                                              CIP

Manufactured in the United States of America
Dover Publications, Inc., 31 East 2nd Street, Mineola, N.Y. 11501

NOTE

This volume presents more than 2,300 illustrations culled from 19th-century sources, offering a broad and authentic overview of the goods and merchandise of the Victorian era. The images have been reproduced directly from rare trade catalogs, as well as from such noted periodicals of the times as *The Illustrated London News, The Art Journal, The Scientific American, Harper's Weekly, Frank Leslie's Illustrated News, The Youth's Companion, Chatterbox, St. Nicholas* and *The Graphic*.

The unprecedented range of goods available to the Victorian-era public was the result of dramatic changes and improvements in manufacturing and transportation brought about by the Industrial Revolution. Better transportation both on land and at sea provided manufacturers with a worldwide market for their products. British companies, for example, could ship their goods to the outermost reaches of the Empire. Settlers in the American West could outfit themselves with a vast array of items ordered from back east. The opening of the world to trade brought a corresponding increase in the demand for products; simultaneous improvements in technology meant that these products could be manufactured quickly and easily, generally making them cheaper and more plentiful. And, with the prosperity that accompanied the Industrial Revolution, more people than ever before were able to afford and enjoy these goods.

The illustrations chosen by Carol Belanger Grafton cover a broad spectrum of products, ranging from the necessary to the luxurious. Herein may be found kitchenware, gardening implements, lanterns and shoes, as well as medicines, walking sticks, jewelry and fans. The technological wonders of the day are represented by cuts of cameras, movie projectors, sewing machines and the like, and the popular pastimes of the day may be discerned from the engravings of roller skates, baseball gloves and bicycles, to mention just a few. The browser will come away from this book with some sense of the tastes and needs of the Victorian consumer, while the designer will find here an invaluable resource for copyright-free spot illustrations with an old-fashioned feeling.

CONTENTS

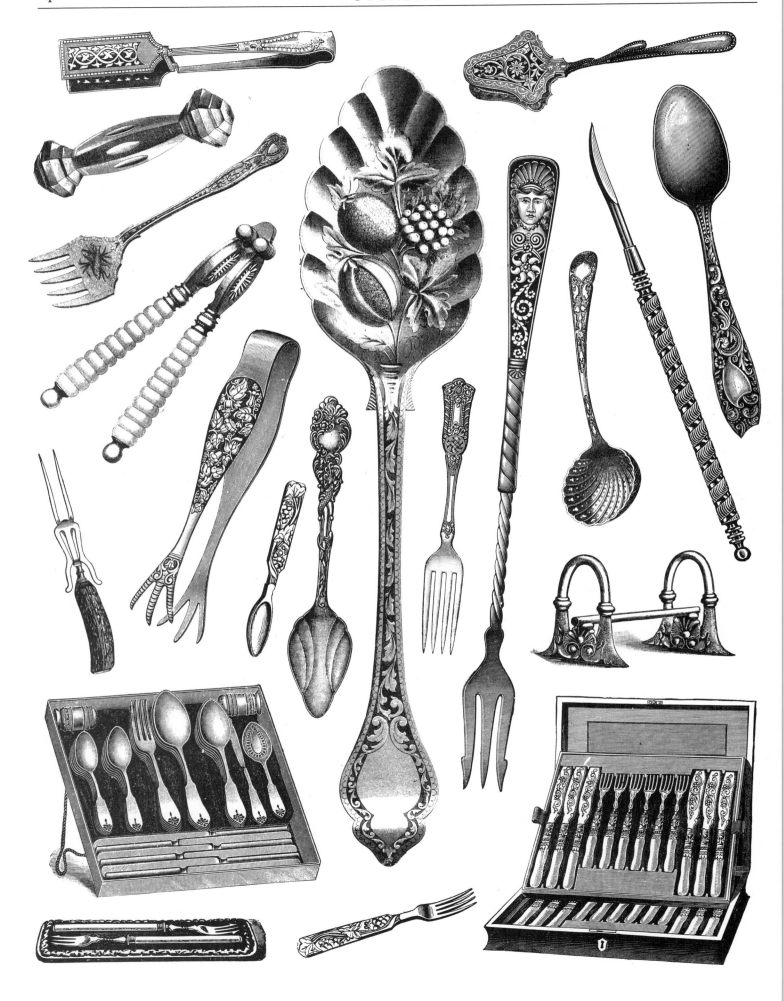

MENU

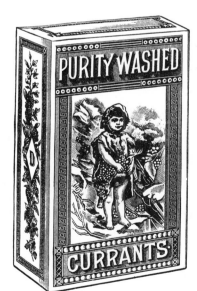

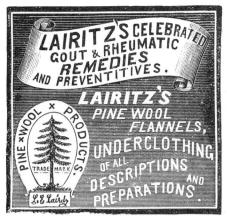

LAIRITZ'S CELEBRATED GOUT & RHEUMATIC REMEDIES AND PREVENTITIVES. LAIRITZ'S PINE WOOL FLANNELS, UNDERCLOTHING OF ALL DESCRIPTIONS AND PREPARATIONS. PINE WOOL PRODUCTS. TRADE MARK.

TARRANT'S SELTZER APERIENT

Dr. BROWN'S Garlic Wafers DYSPEPSIA, HEARTBURN, HEADACHE. PREPARED BY SEARS, ROEBUCK & CO. INC. AND CHICAGO, ILL.

Full directions inside. BRAZILIAN Worm Cakes. PLEASANT AND EFFECTIVE. PREPARED BY SEARS, ROEBUCK INC. AND CO. CHICAGO, ILL.

COMPOUND SUGAR COATED CATHARTIC PILLS

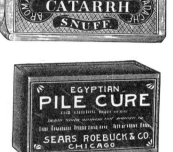

AROMATIC Dr. MARSHALL'S & HEADACHE CATARRH SNUFF.

KOMCHACIN CALORIC For Piles, Hemorrhoids, and Kindred Diseases. 130 Lincoln Street, BOSTON PRICE $1.00. KOMCHACIN CALORIC TRADE MARK. REGISTERED OCT. 11, 1898.

100 GELATINE COATED QUININE PILLS. SEARS ROEBUCK AND CO. CHEAPEST SUPPLY HOUSE ON EARTH CHICAGO, USA.

EGYPTIAN PILE CURE SEARS ROEBUCK & CO. CHICAGO

ENGLISH LAVENDER SALTS PREPARED BY SEARS ROEBUCK & CO. CHICAGO, ILL.

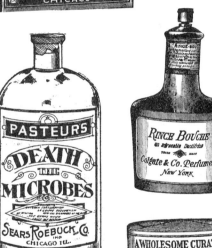

PASTEUR'S DEATH THE MICROBES SEARS ROEBUCK & CO. INC. CHICAGO, ILL.

RINCE BOUCHE an agreeable Dentifrice TRADE MARK Colgate & Co. Perfumers New York

AYER'S CHERRY PECTORAL

WITCH HAZEL JELLY FOR THE SKIN PRICE 25 CENTS MAYELL-HOPP CO. CLEVELAND, O.

THIS SIDE UP THE GREAT SKIN CURE Cuticura GUARANTEED UNDER THE FOOD AND DRUG ACT JUNE 30, 1906 NO. 744. PREPARED BY Potter Drug & Chemical Corp. BOSTON

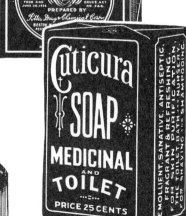

Cuticura SOAP MEDICINAL AND TOILET PRICE 25 CENTS EMOLLIENT, SANATIVE, ANTISEPTIC, FRAGRANT & REFRESHING, FOR SKIN PURIFICATION, FOR THE BATH AND NURSERY, FOR SHAVING.

DR. HOOKER'S COUGH & CROUP SYRUP

OUR $1.50 FAMILY MEDICINE CASE DR. HAMMOND'S HOMEOPATHIC REMEDIES GUARANTEED HIGHEST GRADE MADE SOLD ONLY BY SEARS ROEBUCK AND CO. INC. CHICAGO ILL.

A WHOLESOME CURATIVE THE BEST AND CHEAPEST FOR CONSTIPATION LIVER STOMACH AND BOWEL AILMENTS PRICE 25 CENTS. CONTENTS OF BOTTLE 1200 DROPS DOSES GRADED FROM TWO DROPS FOR INFANTS TO TWO TEASPOONFULS FOR ADULTS PRESCRIBED BY PHYSICIANS AND THE FACULTY. TROPIC FRUIT LAXATIVE Proprietor NEW YORK, U.S.A.

COD LIVER OIL EMULSION WITH HYPOPHOSPHITES A FOOD FOR INFANTS AND INVALIDS SPIERS & POND Ltd. G. W. G. ROBINSON M.P.S. QUEEN VICTORIA STREET, AND WATER LANE E.C.

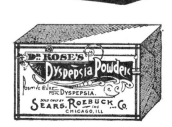

Dr. ROSE'S Dyspepsia Powder POSITIVE CURE FOR DYSPEPSIA. SOLD ONLY BY SEARS, ROEBUCK & CO. INC. CHICAGO, ILL.

CARTER'S LITTLE LIVER PILLS.

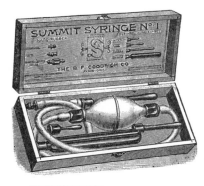

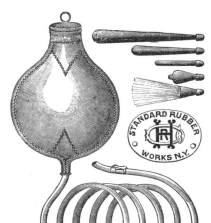

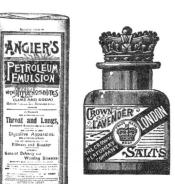

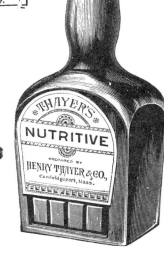

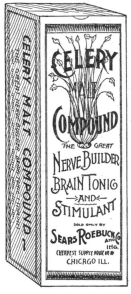

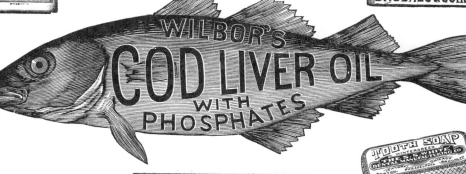

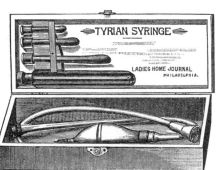

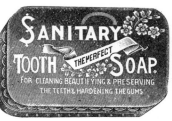

NEW GREEK WINTER ONION

BURPEE'S

TULIPS.

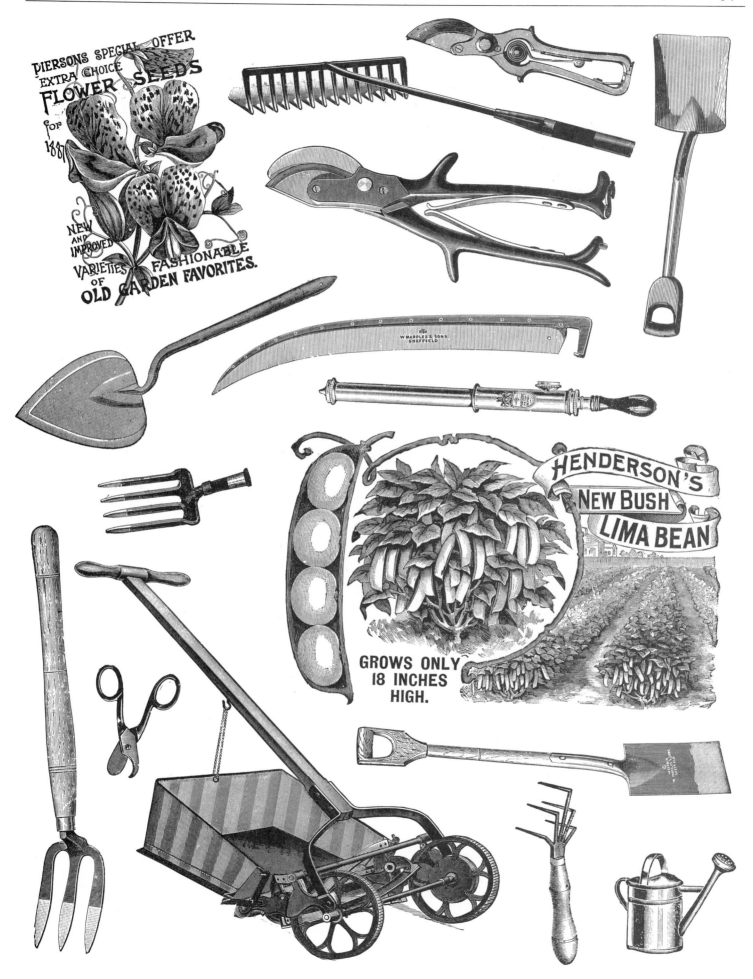

PIERSONS SPECIAL OFFER EXTRA CHOICE FLOWER SEEDS for 1881

NEW AND IMPROVED VARIETIES OF FASHIONABLE OLD GARDEN FAVORITES.

HENDERSON'S NEW BUSH LIMA BEAN

GROWS ONLY 18 INCHES HIGH.

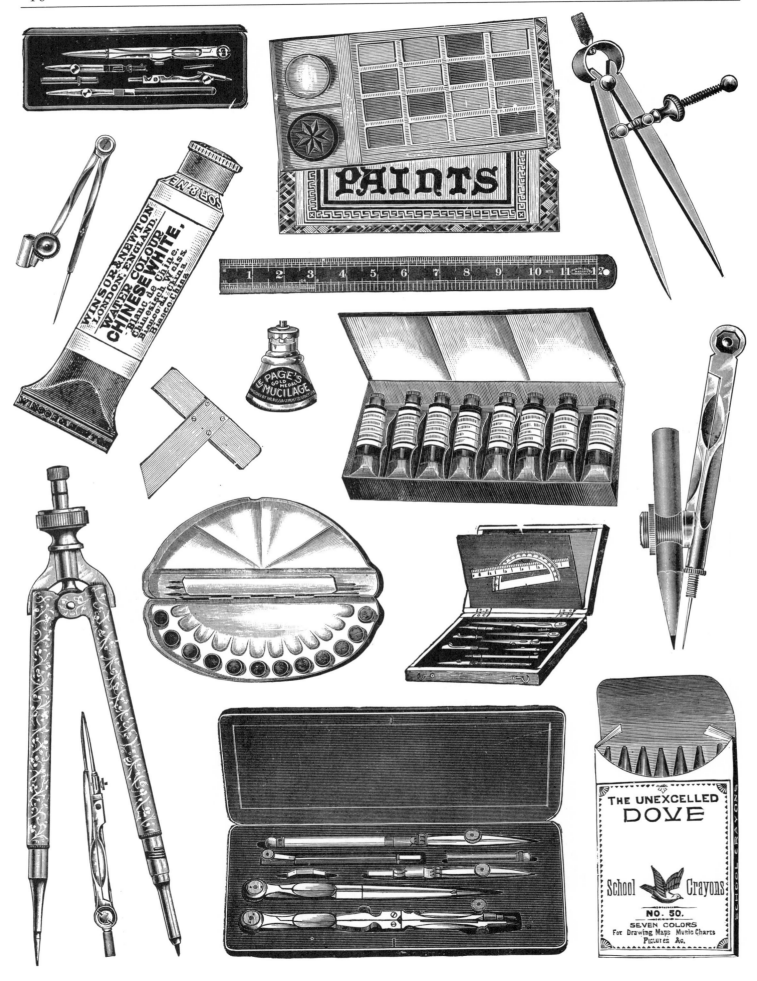

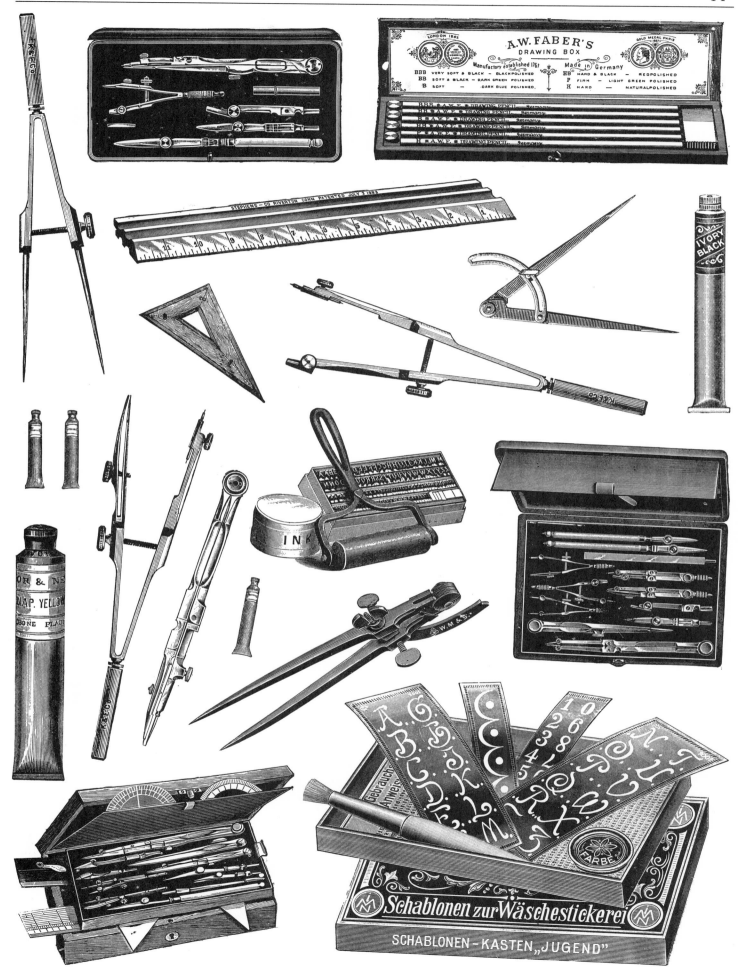

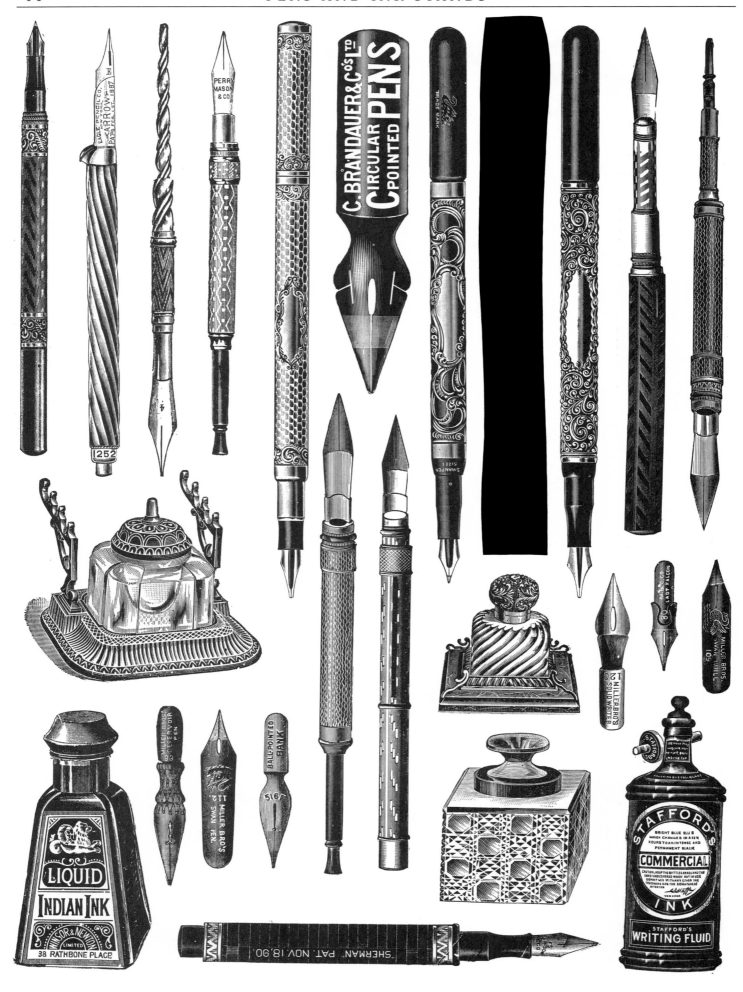

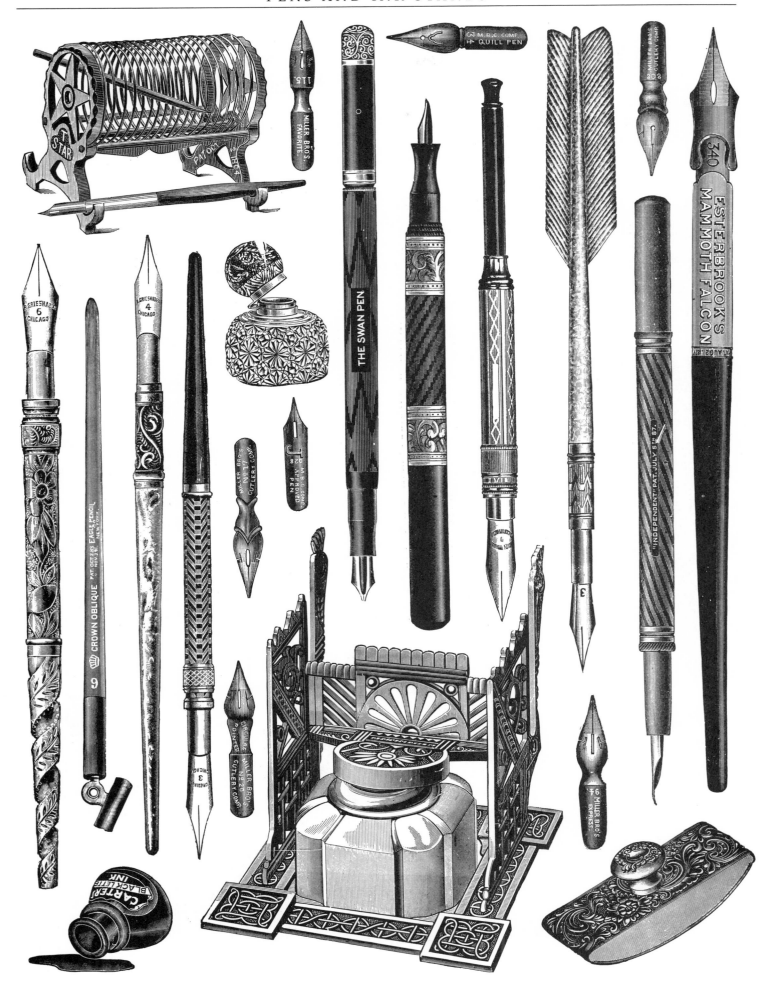

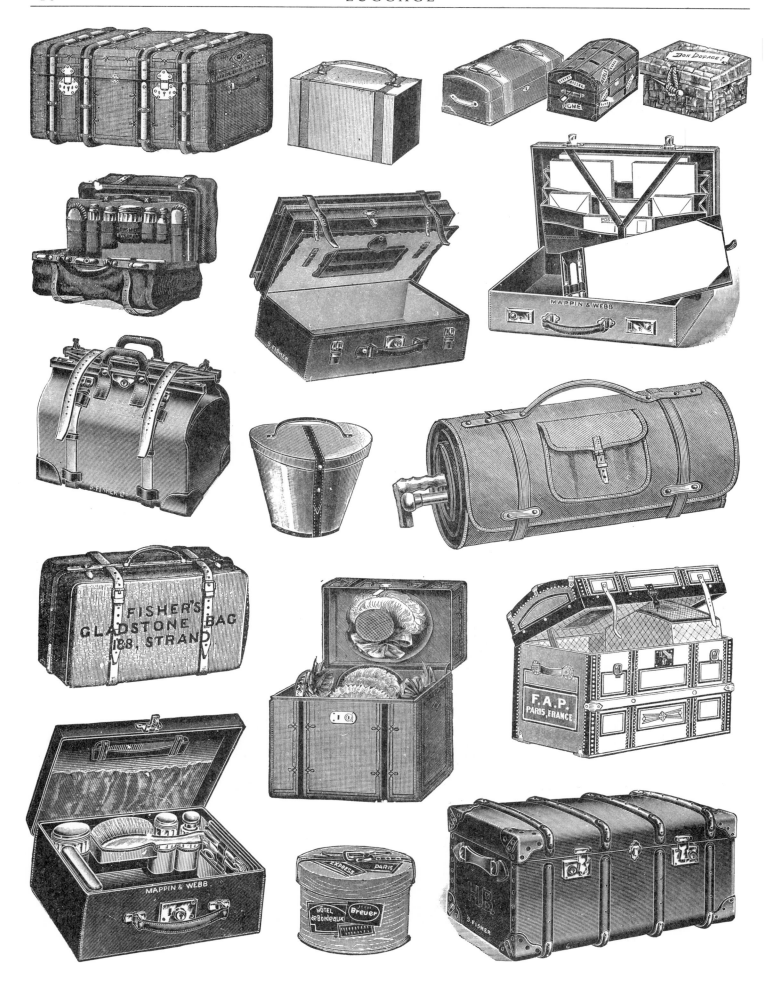

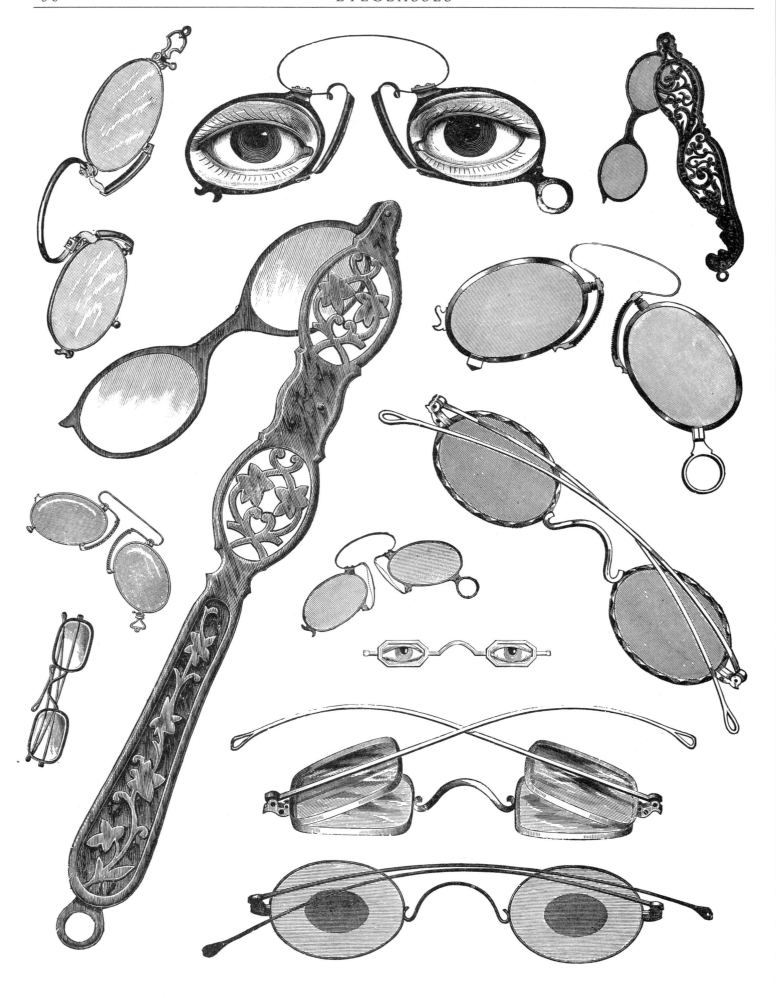

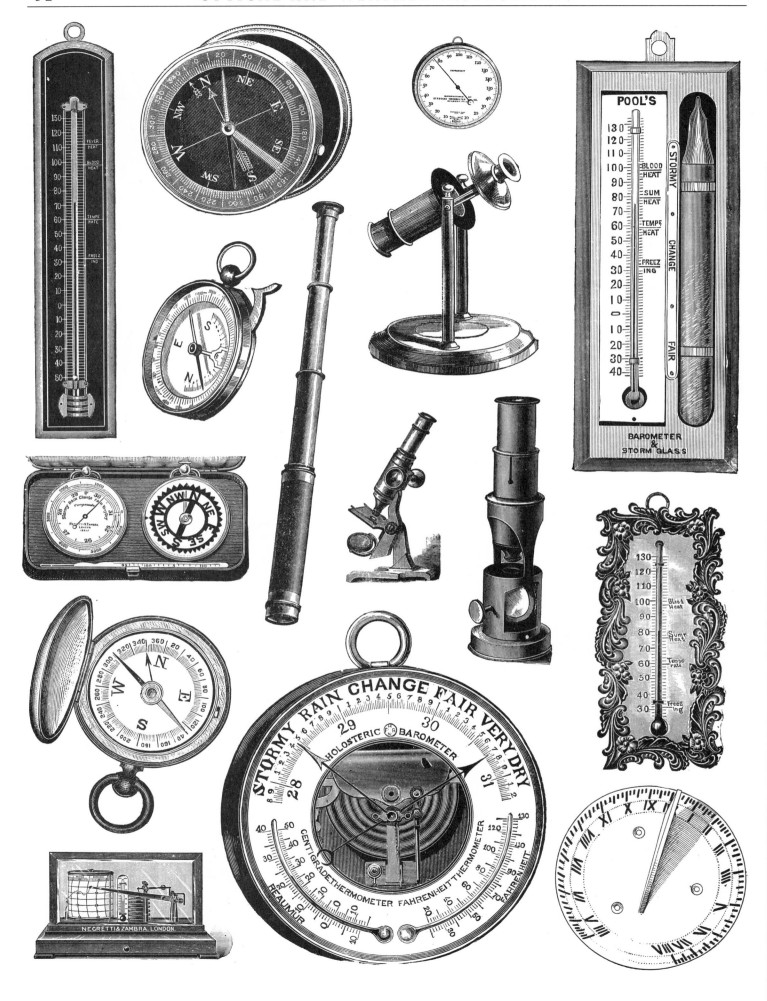

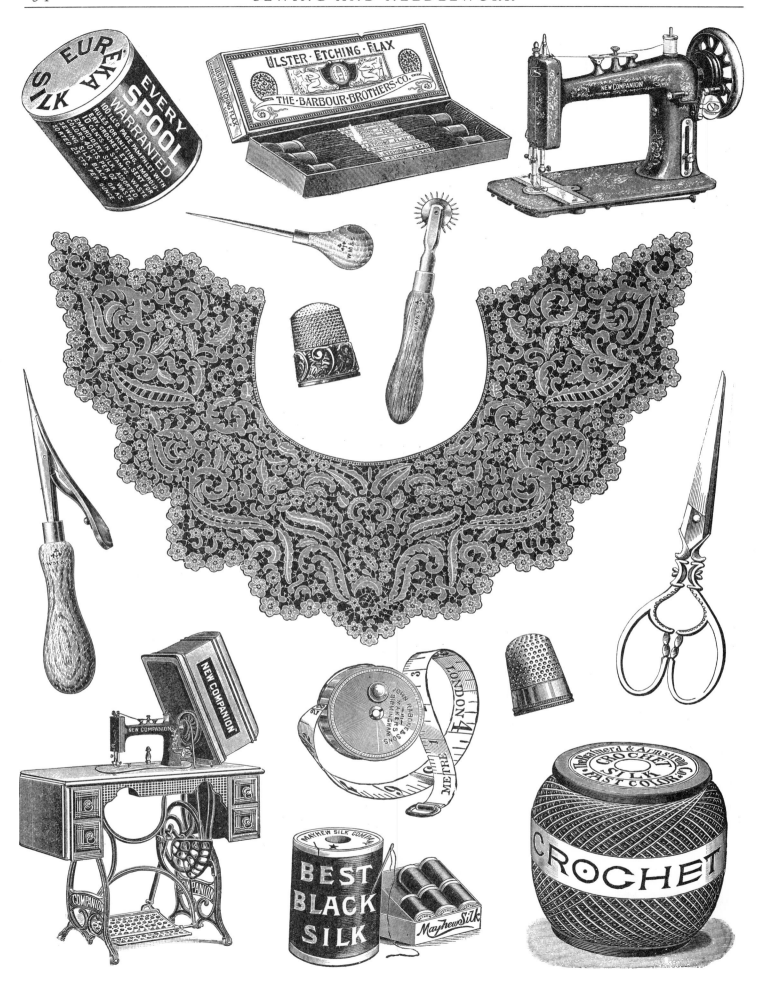

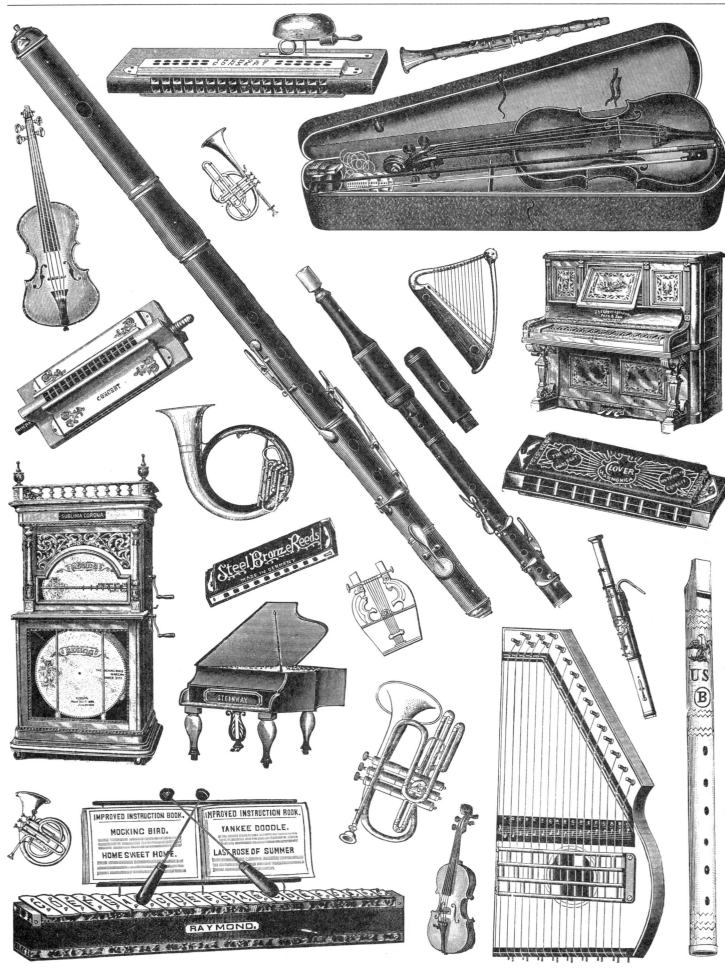

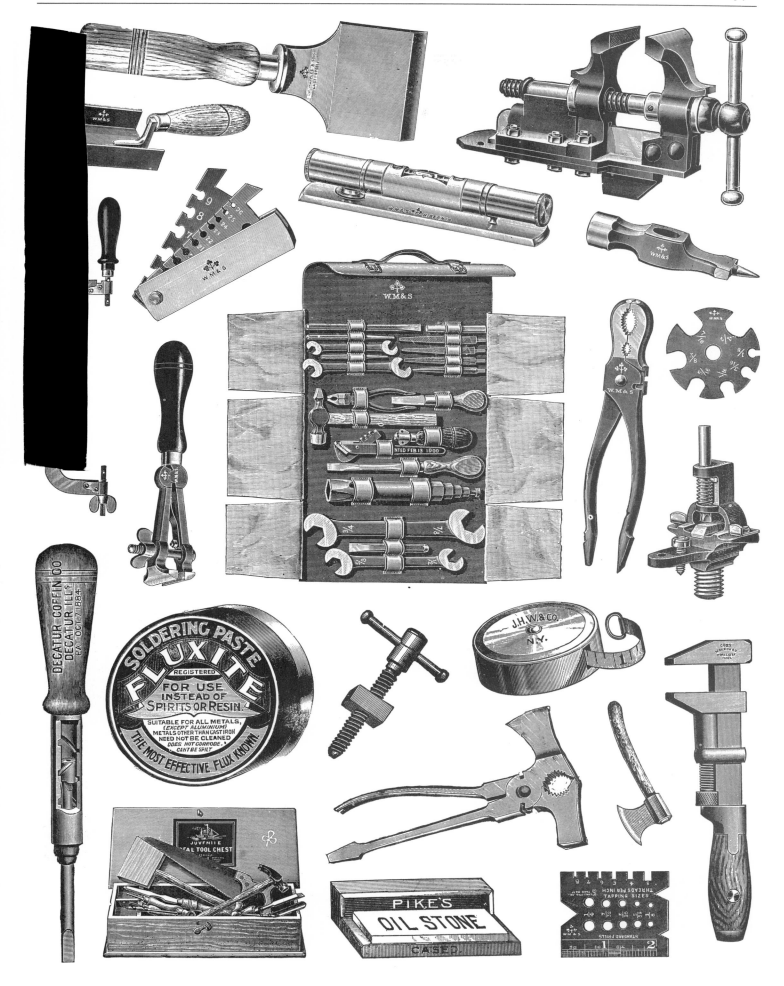

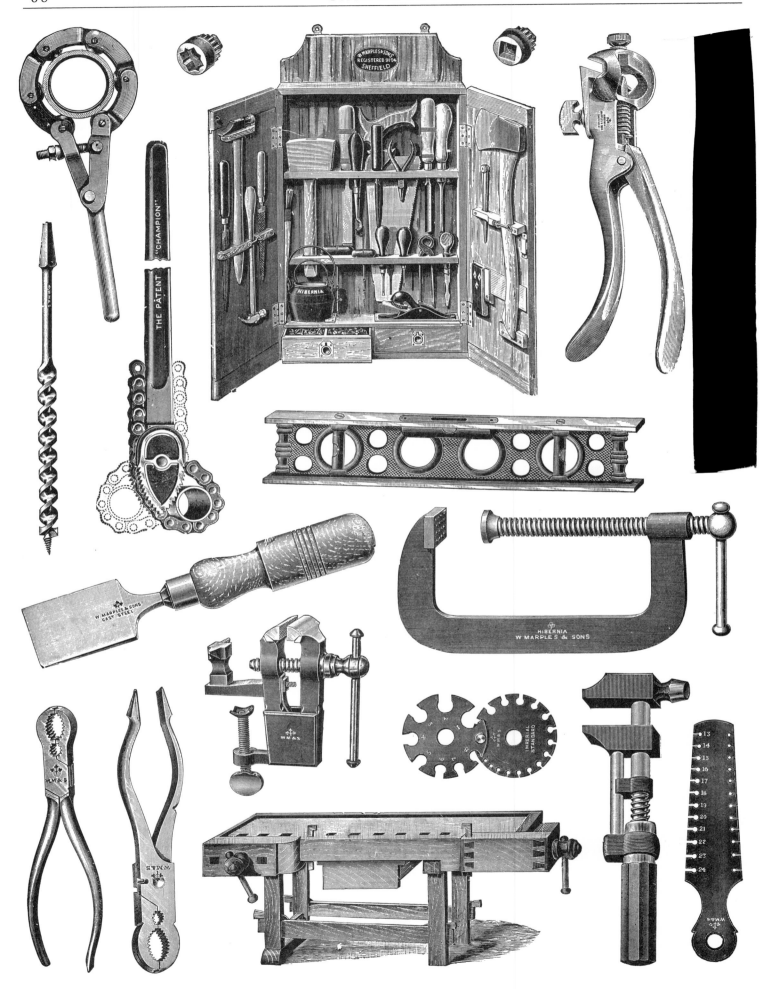

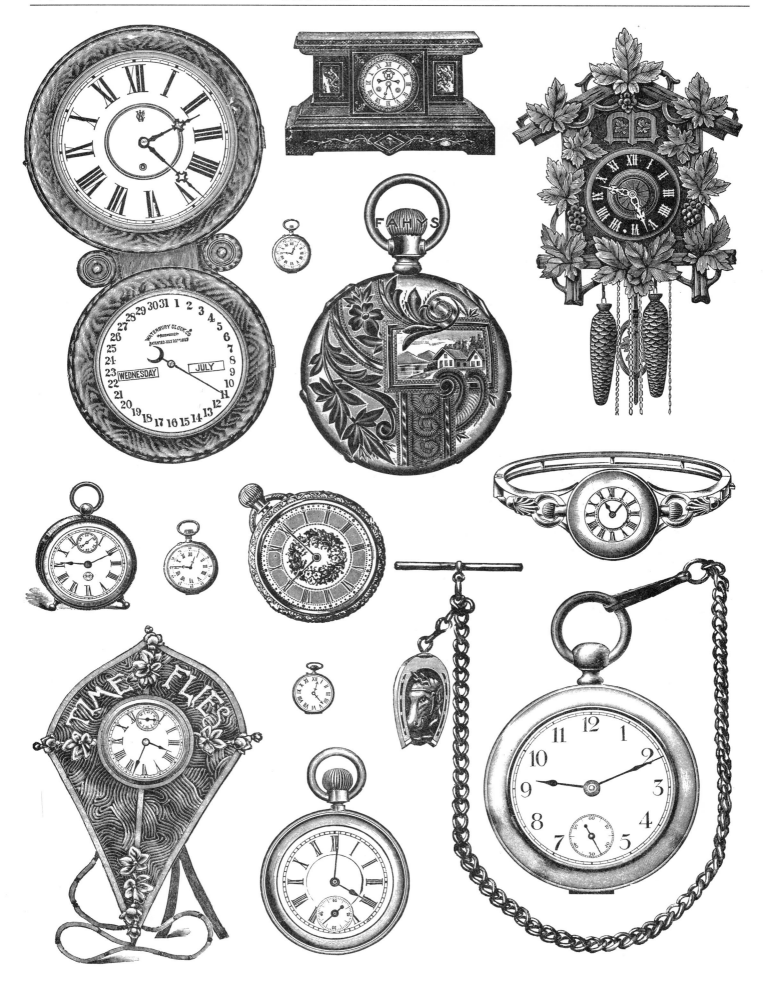

THE WATERBURY WATCH

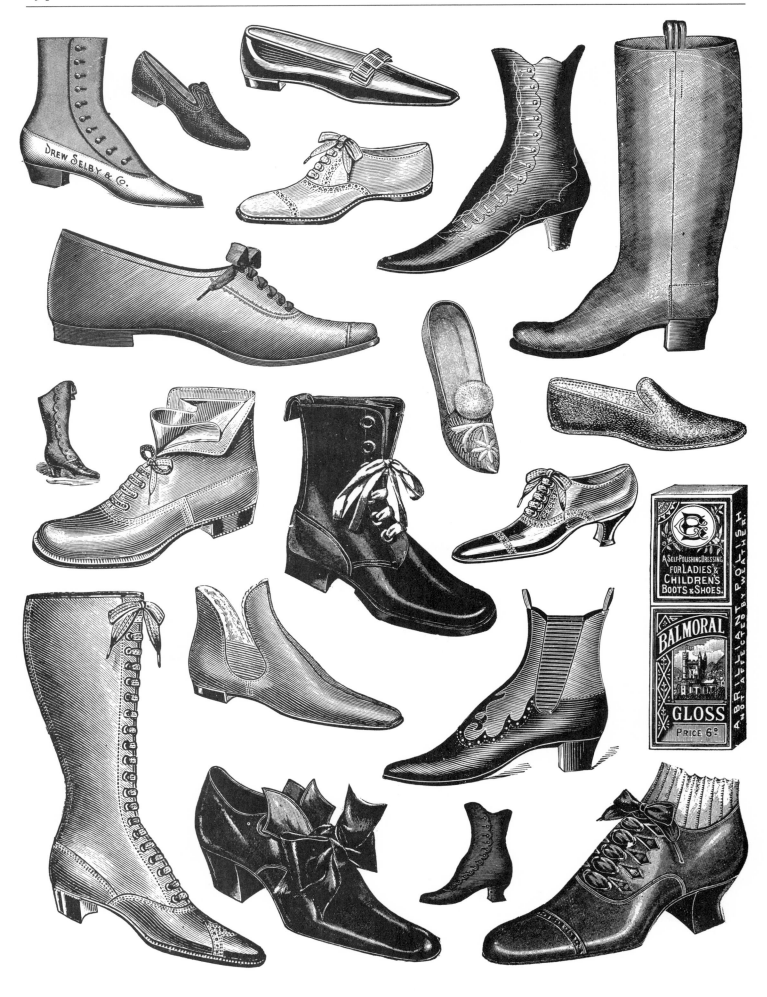

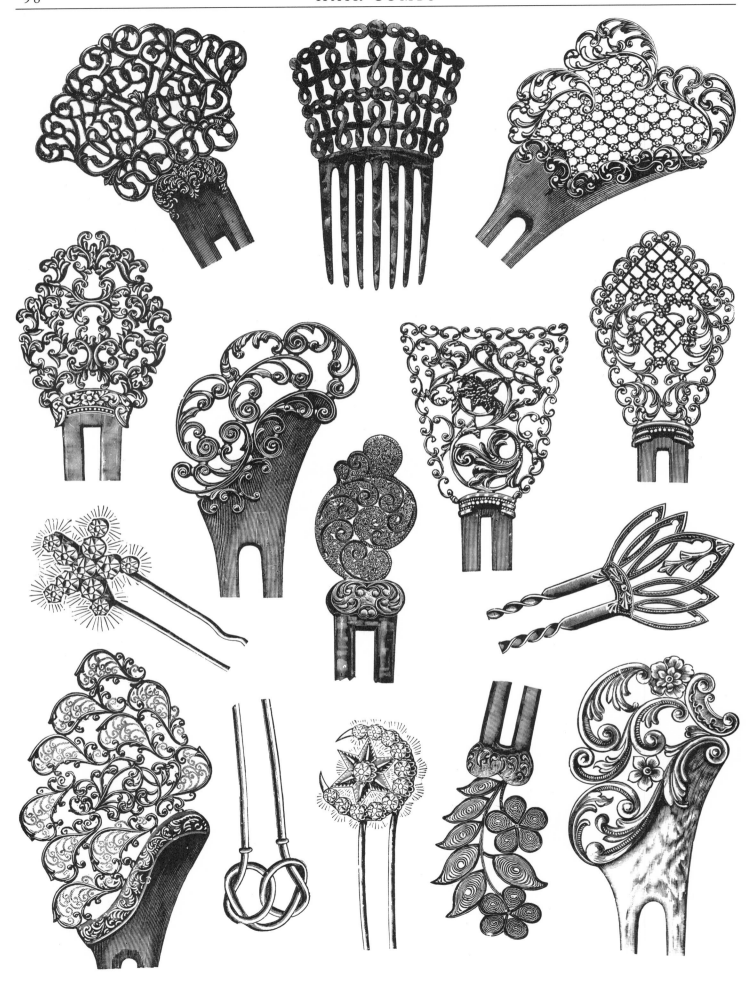

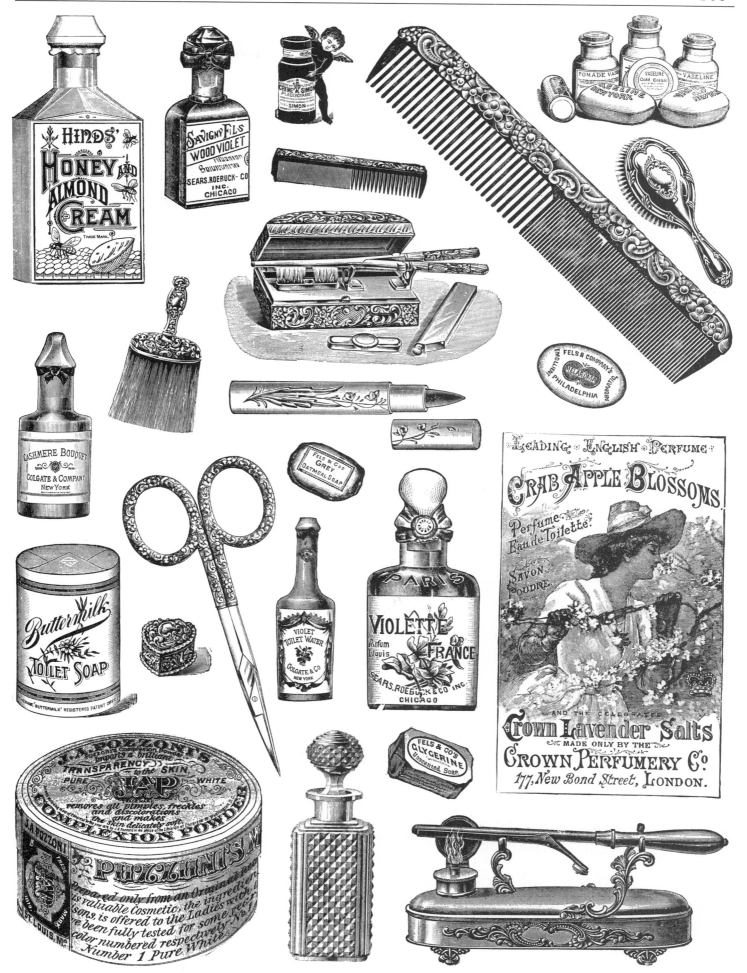

THE
W.H.K & S.
ELLEN TERRY CORSET.

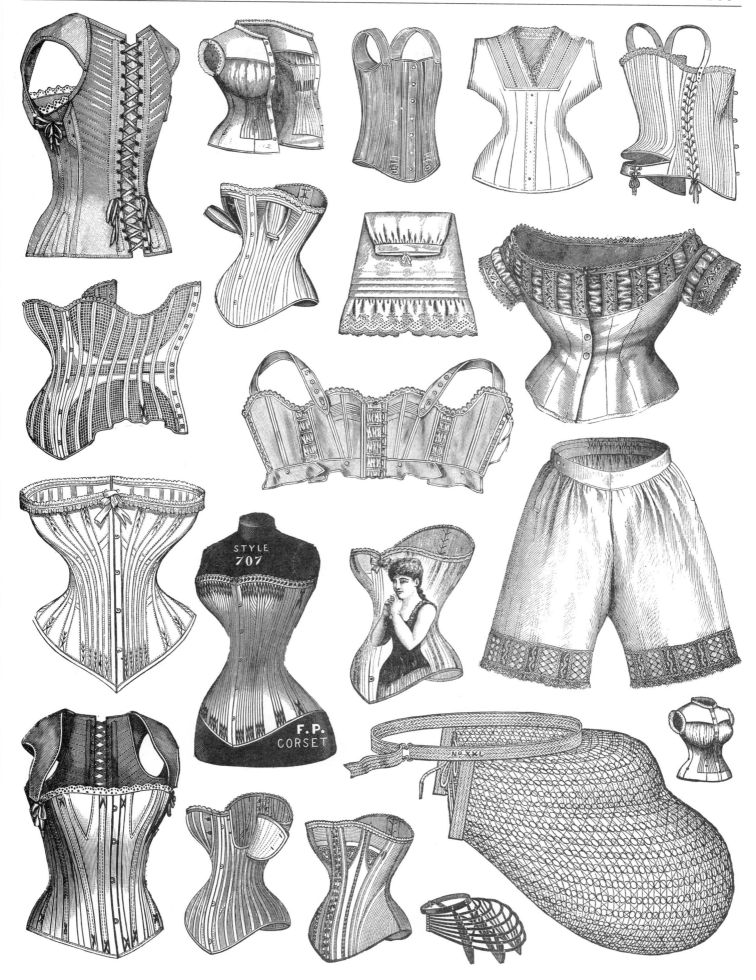

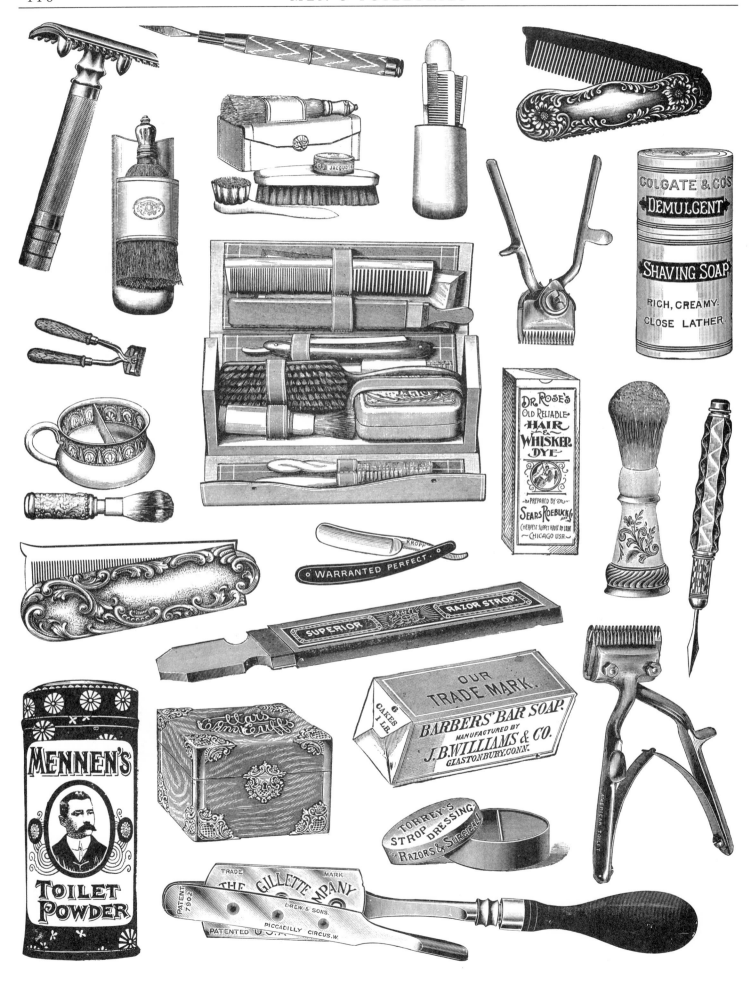

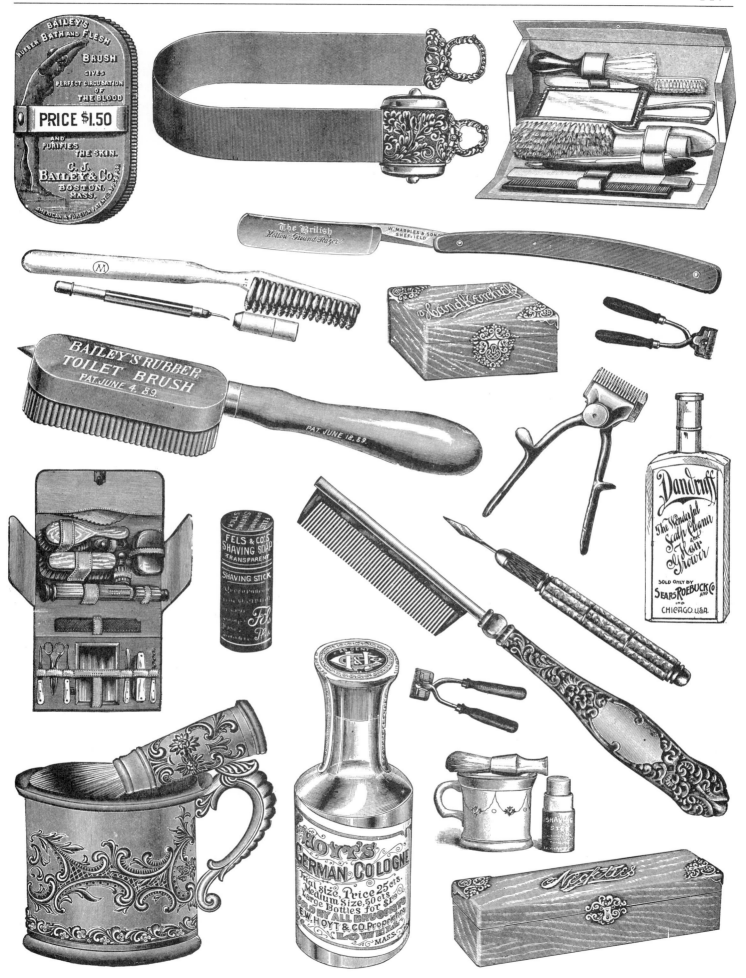